Love's Recipe

A Collection of Poems

by

Terry L. Ware, Sr.

inner child press, ltd.

Credits

Author
Terry L. Ware, Sr.

Editing
Christina Neal
http://www.innerchildpress.com/christina-neal-editing-services.php

Cover Graphic
Chyna Blue ~ edifyin graphix
http://www.innerchildpress.com/edifyin-graphix.php

General Information

Love's Recipe

Terry L. Ware, Sr.

1st Edition : 2013

This Publishing is protected under Copyright Law as a "Collection". All rights for all submissions are retained by the Individual Author and or Artist. No part of this Publishing may be Reproduced, Transferred in any manner without the prior **WRITTEN CONSENT** of the "Material Owner" or its Representative Inner Child Press. Any such violation infringes upon the Creative and Intellectual Property of the Owner pursuant to International and Federal Copyright Law. Any queries pertaining to this "Collection" should be addressed to Publisher of Record.

Publisher Information
1st Edition : Inner Child Press :
intouch@innerchildpress.com
www.innerchildpress.com

This Collection is protected under U.S. and International Copyright Laws

Copyright © 2013 : Terry L. Ware, Sr.
LOC : 1-971080921

ISBN-13 : 978-0615851662
ISBN-10 : 0615851665

$ 16.95

Dedication

I dedicate this book to . . .

my Daughter

Aniah N. Ware

my Son

Terry L. Ware Jr.

Preface

When searching for a title for this book, I prayed and prayed, and prayed. Then one day I could hear the words loud and clear, "Love's Recipe". This title defined what I wanted to capture within my first book, and all that is involved when we choose to love.

I want those who pick up this book and read through the lines of poetry to be intrigued by the words as they express the ins and outs of love. I pray that this book will be a help to those who are searching for answers. May it enlighten you and enrich you and give you a new outlook on love.

All in all I pray that you enjoy it.

Terry L. Ware Sr.

Foreword

Love's recipe is not something you will find in anyone's cookbook. It's a tradition passed down from one generation to the next. It is passed from parents to children through displays of affection, through working together to achieve like goals, and supporting one another's passions, child-rearing and discipline. Love is a mixture of family game nights, dinner conversations, help with homework, and vacations. WE watch and emulate what we've seen, remove what may not be to our particular tastes, and, when it's time, prepare it in our own homes, with our own families. Love is a tradition, habitual and genetic.

In this collection, Terry Ware takes love and breaks it down to its core elements: the good and the bad. He stirs up memories of what we've seen and heard from childhood on into our own present existences. He makes you smile, blush, cry, and pause, even if briefly, to consider what can be done differently. This collection shows that good times can become great and bad times can get better. He also gives the harsh reminder that there is a very thin line between bliss and misery. Terry makes you acknowledge that the scales can be tipped at any given moment.

I urge you to read this collection at least three times. Once for enjoyment, twice for education, and three times for edification. Take in every word. The seamless flow of the writing, and the lessons it provides, respectively.

Though all poets begin writing for themselves, it is proven, in this work that the universal purpose of poetic creation is to serve us all.

After your third ingestion, sit back with a pen and pad, and document your own recipe.

Jamesha Miner Henderson

Poetic Advisory, LLC

Table of Contents

Preface	vii
Foreword	viii
Guidance	1
Love - Can I Look At You?	2
Quiet Time	4
A Diamond in the Rough	5
All Out of Options	7
Connected	8
Imitation Love	9
If God Cried	10
Intangible Love	12
I Took My Last Breath	13
Mind Over Matter	14
Taylor Made	15
Tears of Prayer	16
Act Like a Man, Think Like a Woman	17
The Re-birth	18
Turn the Page	20
Unbreakable Love	22
My Protection	23
Lost Love	24
Let Go and Live	26

Table of Contents ... *continued*

Journey	27
Love in a Moment	28
It's Ok	29
Flesh of My Flesh, Bone of My Bone	30
Hypothetically Speaking	31
I Apologize	33
I Dreamed As I Walked	35
Advice Un-trusted	36
All of Me	37
A Father's Love	38
As I Look In the Sky	40
How Can I Breathe	41
How Did I Get Here ~ Love	43
How Did I Get Here ~ Life	45
I'm Dreaming	47
If Not Me Then Who	49
I Wish	50
I Was Distracted For a Brief Moment	51
You Raped Me	52
Circular Emotions	54
Contact	55
Definition of a Man	56

*T*able of *C*ontents . . . *continued*

From My Heart to Yours	58
I'm In Search of but I'm Not Looking	59
I Am Not What I Was	61
I Could, But Why	62
I Got a Jones	63
I Never Knew You	65
Consequences of Actions	66
Unconditional	67
What I See	68
When I Met You	69
When It's Your Fault	71
When Love Is Lost	73
Don't Wanna	75
Emotional Roller Coaster	76
Finally In Love	78
Focus	80
From My Heart to Yours	81
Life's Renovation	82
Love Letter to Self	84
Love	85
Love's Promise	86
Life and Love	87

Table of Contents . . . *continued*

Little Feelings of Love	88
Love or Lust	90
It's Time	92
Mirage	96
Loving Is Not Being in Love	97
Moving Forward	98
My Angel	99
My Soul Bleeds	101
New World	103
No Goodbyes	105
My Children	106
My God	108
No Regrets	109
Our Day	111
Overdosed	112
Quiet Storm	114
Same Ol Love Song	115
Sweet Unity	117
Since We Last Spoke	118
Stop Lying	119
The Essence of True Love	121
Suicide Love	123

Table of Contents... continued

The Pain I Feel	125
The Night We Kissed	127
The Perfect Night	129
Through the Clutter	130
Thoughts of the Heart	131
Where Is Your Protection	134
What's This Feeling	136
So Amazing	138
Am I in Love	139
How Do I Stay	140
My Queen	142
Permanent Love	143
The Very Essence of a Blessing	144
Love's Recipe	146
Epilogue	149
About the Author	151
A Few Words from Terry	152

Epilogue

about the Author	151
a few words from Terry	152
Connections to Terry	153

Terry L. Ware, Sr.

Love's Recipe

A Collection of Poems

by

Terry L. Ware, Sr.

inner child press, ltd.

Love's Recipe

Guidance

Moving through the night my eyes blinded by the depths of this world

Will I be able to find my way through all this misery without the feeling to hurl

Pain, hunger, and frustration all lay ahead, traps of Satan wanting us all to fall dead

No time to stop, no time to pause, gotta keep moving, His name I shall always call

Help me, hold me, understand that I need You, and most importantly understand that I breathe You

For without You my life is only sand, Lord God, I am willing to take a stand

Not only for myself, but for those who don't believe, forgiveness for them I beg and plead

Hear my cry, but dry my tears, for You said in Your word that You will always be near

Faith of a mustard seed You said is all I need, and your blessings You shall pour from heaven is what I will need to feed

Fear not, want not, I travel not alone, for my father Jesus will one day take me home

Terry L. Ware, Sr.

Love - Can I Look At You?

Beautifully amazing, extravagantly precious, full of emotions, a bond that should be unbreakable

Just a few words that briefly explain you

Yet it seems I've always held you as a tool

You have been in and out of my life time and time again

But instead of my lover for life, you've always ended up my friend

I cherish you as a friend, yet, this time is not how I want it to end

It's time I search deep within you, for something about you I am missing

This time, this time I have endeavored to take the time out to listen

I want you to touch my mind with the inner part of your soul

So that all your ins and outs I can make a part of me

That I will never hurt you, misuse you, nor take your life for granted

The simplest thing about you I desire to know, for that is what makes you

Love's Recipe

I want to search your heart so that your pains become my pains, and your hurts, my hurts

I need to examine you to know all your curves, your bruises, your feelings, so that I can learn how to embrace you

I need you but can't have you till I have looked at you

I have only touched you but never held onto you

You see, I need to look at you, for if I never take the time to look at you, entrap myself within you,

How will I ever be able to hold on to you

How can I make you a part of my life for an eternity

How can I make you feel as special as you are

If I never take time out to look at you

Terry L. Ware, Sr.

Quiet Time

Thinking becomes easy
Time seems to slow down
Blood seems to flow
Evenly from head to toe
This is my quiet time

Shut out to everything else
One focus
One mind
One breath
This is my quiet time

No sounds
No distractions
No feelings of obligations
No limits
This is my quiet time

No internet
No music
No kids
No grown-ups acting as kids
This is my quiet time

During this time
There is nothing to fear
All his thoughts I endeavor to hear
As he talks
Purification comes over my soul
It's only Him and I
And this is His time
This is my quiet time

A Diamond in the Rough

Many obstacles I face

Yet still determined to see His face

Knocked down a many of times

Above all I will always rise

Kicked from behind

Seems as if I'm losing ground

He sees the best in me

While others talk and ridicule me

Determined I will always be

Though my destiny at times I just can't see

From hardships to mind flips

Still you can't have me, on His Grace I'll continue to sip

Many nights filled with tears

Holding on to strength because He said fear I should never feel

Terry L. Ware, Sr.

Guaranteed to be a winner, as long as I never let go

With strength comes more room to grow

So let the rain continue to fall

He'll never put more on me, even though at times I stall

A diamond in the rough I just may be

But watch how I'll shine once He is finished with me!!!

All Out of Options

Frustrated with pain that fills my emotions

Indulged within the changes that my life faces

Seemingly unknowing from one day to the next

Keeps me from guessing remaining perplexed

Still and yet

Strong I must remain

Keeps my mind from being reframed

Detained to only those solutions

Clouded by other's transfusions

Yet

No connections just illusions

Mind frustrated with the lack of a thought

Depending on others leaves me distraught

A key plan

Yeah

That's what I need

Never out of options

For outstretched is always His hand

Awaiting me to grab

Terry L. Ware, Sr.

Connected

You weren't my first love
I never even looked your way
In school from you
I always strayed
You appealed to me
But I just figured
With you
I'd never be
Undeniably
I felt you were far beyond me
You and me
Man I just couldn't see
But now you and me
Apart I just can't see
Your blood now runs through mine
Dipped in wine
Our relationship gets finer with time
Whether I found you
Or you found me
It's irrelevant really
Because now in this world
There's not just you
Not just me
It's simply we
You have become a part of my lifeline
Without you
A part of me would just die
The gift of poetry
Yeah
It's my lifestyle

Imitation Love

Questions that circle in my mind

Leaves false pretences behind

For everything you said

You never did

For everything you claimed to be

I must have been blinded for I've never seen

What lined your heart is what really showed

Maybe love your heart just couldn't hold

To console

You tried

Attempts

Denied

Mostly because fake-ism is what resigned

Your eyes showed the most

For they were the host

Your ears consumed with frustrations

Listening to others caused you hesitations

Simply put

The reasons you couldn't reach your destination

What's left, simply an imitation!!!

Terry L. Ware, Sr.

If God Cried

Hurt from constant false promises
Declarations that were meaningless
The 'if you's, and 'I's
The 'next time's that are a false pretence
For the un-realization of what love really is
Surely this causes God to cry
And if God cried, shouldn't we feel His pain?

The constant pressure from being used
As a tool that we only pull out when we need it
When we need, we constantly go to You
The denominator being constant
While the numerator is You
The equalization is an unlimited
Number of times that You we use
Surely this causes God to cry
And if God cried, shouldn't we feel His pain?

Love's Recipe

The mistreatment of His word
We most times use it as a curve
We say God is love
But, when in tight situations, we show no love
Instead we shove Him aside and depend on an alternate guide
Wondering why we fall deeper and deeper into the opinions of those we confide
Inside they too have decided to hide
Which is why they can't find the trueness that they need
So, on their opinions, You they continue to feed
Surely this causes God to cry
And if He cried shouldn't we feel His pain?

We say inside of us is where God lives
But if one searched, what would they actually find
Of Him would there be any sign
Surely this causes God to cry
And if He cried, how would we feel His pain
If we continue to use him in vain?!!!

Terry L. Ware, Sr.

Intangible Love

This love I have never felt
This love face to face I have never seen
This love have I only dreamed
The way I feel inside leaves me speechless
To the point where I find my meekness
This love is desirable
This love is pleasurable
This love, this love leaves no wounds
This love only comforts
This love constantly consoles
This love is what I desire to hold
This love is honest
This love is modest
This love is what everyone claims to have,
yet no one has proven
This love brings sunshine in the midst of the rain
This love wipes all tears away when pain seems to stay
This love makes sense and lets me know here I can stay
This love seems to make no mistakes
This love seems perfect in everyway
This love, when times are hard, takes you through with ease
This love in no way is hard to please
This love one day will I find?
This love, when it approaches, I will recognize

I Took My Last Breath

It was at the very moment my eyes graced yours
I knew because around there was no one
In a room filled with many bodies
It was your soul that pinched my pupils
As if he himself touched
Mr. Cupid

There were no second thoughts
No what ifs
No buts
No "What if she's not the one?"
It was like my mind froze in time
Because when I came to
You were mine

Standing there with that amazing smile
Pearly whites were white as snow
The room bright as you shined from head to toe
Peculiar I was to know
So I leaned in kissing you gently, slow
Yeah, just what I already knew
At that moment I breathed my last breath
And began to breathe you!!!!!!!

Mind Over Matter

Could it be possible to know my name

Could it be possible to lose the game

Could it be possible to hold a meaningful conversation

Could it be possible that what lies beneath my clothes is not your destination

Could it be possible to look in my eyes when we speak

Could it be possible that my assets is not what made you speak

Could it be possible to get to know me for me

Could it be possible that you're not just inspired by what you see

Could it be possible that respect means just that, respect

Could it be possible that the respect isn't just until you hit

Could it be possible that I'm worth more than your money

Could it be possible that you not feel obligated to prove you have lots of money

Could it be possible that maybe I am your dream

Could it be possible that you would know if only you had taken the time and not gone off what I seemed

Love's Recipe

Taylor Made

Designed specifically, nothing like others
Fitted to the t, made just for me
Your mind coincides with thoughts within me
Though hidden deep inside, your thoughts consume me
Many have come along, yet I've always felt alone
Trying to make them what I thought they should be
Only to find wasted time through my stressed out mind
Thoughts blinded with love in front of me as you stood
there, past you I couldn't see
Made up love to fill my emotionless capacity
Trying to find rest within an imaginative reality
The real me no one could see,
yet I strived to be all they wanted me to be
Never understanding, left contemplating
just what was wrong with me
My eyes have now been opened, and very clearly I now see
You were there blocking the false love
that wasn't meant for me
No matter who came along,
the real me they would never see
Since my thoughts were not your thoughts
clearly my mind couldn't focus
For the destination of my landing
could only be safe with you
Like a suit made to perfectly fit the one it was designed
I am thankful that my perfect fit I have now found

Terry L. Ware, Sr.

Tears of Prayer

I shed a tear last night

Not because I wanted to, but rather I had to

I shed a tear last night

Knowing this love I have for you

I shed a tear last night

For the pain that runs within you

I shed a tear last night

Because of all that you are going through

I shed a tear last night

Blessed in my life to have had you

I shed a tear last night

Feeling lost for words and none to find

I shed a tear last night

Not knowing if your love again I would ever find

I shed a tear last night

Because it pains me to let you go

I shed a tear last night

Knowing by morning you would be gone

I shed a tear last night

As my sign became light

Love's Recipe

Act Like a Man, Think Like a Woman

Stand up for you now
But keep in mind she's looking at how you stand

Speak truth rather than lies
Remember your actions should never hide
Keep in mind your words float past her
It's your actions that grab her

Sure you can cheat
And she may never find out
But keep in mind through intuition she knows
Though she may never tell you she knows

Listen closely to her every word
For it's through her words that expressions of life you can find
But keep in mind at some time
She's going to want you to recite those words

Take care of her
Protect her
Let her know you are her man
But keep in mind she'll be expecting you to be just that
Her man
Speak well of her
Even in those times she gets on your nerves
Keep in mind that it's what you say that will either escalate or calm her

If you show and act like the man
Know that every part of that woman
Will compliment all of that man

Terry L. Ware, Sr.

The Re-birth

My hopes and dreams turned into a reality the day I met You

Thoughts of being secure, free, with a piece of serenity

Never lacking that trust factor because, for me, You were always there, even when I wasn't there for me

For every situation I contemplated which direction I would take next

Never realizing that my next was within You, if only I would confide in You

Mind boggling, clouded tears, feet that constantly hurt because I walked further away from You

My skin sore for the lack of blood that once flowed because of You

Desperation became my proclamation trying to reach my destination without You

I lost sight of You as I drifted into the night, no sunlight for guidance just me trying to feel my way through

Behind every action is a reaction and I reacted to the things around me

See, that trust I once knew in You now seemed hidden because I choose to turn away from You

The love that I once found in You remained in You, but for me was nowhere to be found

Love's Recipe

Now, seemingly stuck at the end of my journey, yes I said seemingly, it's as if my life has been doomed
But just an ounce of what's left in me tells me that my only way out is to look to You
Suffer little children to come under You. I've suffered now
I humble myself as a child, bow down and come into You
Wrap me in your arms, console me, mold me, re-conform me
I replace my life in You so that I may regain life
Breathing a fresh breath of air brings the color back to my skin
Knowing I have You on the inside, falling in love with You, lets me know, no matter what, I will always win!

Terry L. Ware, Sr.

Turn the Page

Destiny had no place
Everywhere I moved seemed to be erased
To say the wrong thing
It was just a matter of time
No disrespect intended
Just wasn't feeling the ground
Moving around
Seemingly in circles
Sometimes at a standstill
Never once did I feel
Those things you said you felt
Often asked why
But left with tears that filled my eyes
Within those tears I wanted to drown
Clown
Big nose, big feet
Mixed colors as I walked through the streets
Yeah, that's how I felt
Out of place
And if you seen me
I'm sure you would have laughed
But
That's because the outside you would've seen
Missing the pain that seemingly blocked my dreams
Felt as if defeat was my life style
No matter where I turned I would never make it out
Was I blind
Was I losing my mind
I couldn't understand it
Or maybe I just didn't try hard enough
What I didn't see
What I couldn't see

Love's Recipe

As if I was buried twenty feet deep
But then
Reality set in with three simple words
Turn. The. Page.
See hardships we never plan
They even make us feel less than a man
A woman
But one thing we have to know
In this life the key is in our hands
The saddest thing is
We remain locked up
Constantly looking at the key
For fear of change
So desperate to remain the same
Not realizing that the same = no gain
No new ground
No new air
That's why we say life's isn't fair
The truth is moving forward, is becoming rare
So the question is
What in your life is your page
And are you willing to be strong
Are you willing
To turn the page!!!!!

Unbreakable Love

Held at a standard never to be disposed of no matter how much pain it feels
Seeing through the hardest of times, the deepest of fears
Many times carrying burdens that last for years and years
Smiling in the midst of situations when it seems no end to the frustrations
Driven by passions unknown, immune to the passiveness by which we sometimes call home
Very rare of its kind, thinks through the soul and never the mind
All of what we dream, yet most have never seen
Searching deep within ourselves at times getting lost through the feelings of no one cares
Many roads we've traveled, trips ripped apart for what we thought was pleasing to the eyes
Left scorn as though we had no feelings inside
Still it moves from day to day from one to the next
Hoping each time that within us it can find rest
Bodies clouded with mentalizations of past hurts
Seeming to push it along leaving us feeling lower than dirt
At times it's as if our lives are inconsolable
For hard knock ways seem to control us
But how precious life would be with a love that's unbreakable

My Protection

Over and over again, it seems there is no end

Love never stays, only passes by and stares at me in a daze

I wish upon a star, yet my dreams remain just that, dreams

As time has gone on, so has my protection

It is built by the pain that surrounds my life

It is held together by the frustrations that bring strife

My protection blocks out that which is not strong enough to maintain

It is my safe zone, and this place no one has called home

Until I find that one that is willing to climb and conquer my soul

My protection will remain my wall

Terry L. Ware, Sr.

Lost Love

Where do I begin, this pain I feel I wish would end

You walk around like nothing is going on

Like what you are doing is absolutely not wrong

The words you speak to me cut deep as a knife

Every night I cry and cry and cry, wishing I would just die

I haven't done anything wrong so why is it I'm the one that feels so alone

I remember how things use to be, how you would often spend a lot of time with me

Now my time has shifted to that of your new love

I'm truly not understanding and my mind just will not comprehend

How did I become second to a bottle of gin

It seems like every time you come home, that's the first thing you greet

No' hello's, or 'how you doing's

Just you and your bottle plopped in your favorite seat

Love's Recipe

How much more can I possibly take, is what I constantly ask myself

Late at night when I am ready to get down in the bed

One look at you and my emotions become dead

My life seems like its slowly day to day slipping away

But I refuse to sit back, and with my life, you have your way

I am somebody, and this somebody is leaving you today

No 'please don't go's, or 'how can I leave you's

Because with you

Your new love will remain

And without you

Your old love will be whole again

Terry L. Ware, Sr.

Let Go and Live

It seems at times we come across people in our lives whom we care for so much, and it seems they are all we can think about.

Yet, it seems the past keeps creeping in and you can't fully concentrate on the things that really matter.

Instead, you compare past things on different situations that happen at hand, when really, everything that you think is happening in your own mind.

The devil wants you to believe that you are never going to be loved, you will never be taken serious, or you will never find that special person you are looking for because they don't exist.

So tell me, are you going to continue to live in the past and make it as the devil is correct or, can you face the possibility that this is real?

Will you be able to understand that every situation is different, that maybe this time it's the real thing?

We can't possibly know the future or when God will send us that right one. But what we can do is take our time in every situation. I promise you that though you may have doubts at first deep down inside, you will feel when it is right.

So in every situation you must let go of what has happened in your past, and live for what is at hand…!

Journey

Unknown destination
Holding on only to hope
Declaring with each situation you will cope
Through each failure
Through every frustration
No one seems to know
Never giving up
Determined no matter what you will go
Seemingly endless ways to turn
But to turn means the possibility to be burned
Up
Down
Forward
Backward
Side to side
Pulled in every direction
Yet, and still, because of your faith
Problems are not a reflection of who you are
Steadfast, unmovable
Yeah, that's what describes you
Based on His love
You never have to stand alone
For it is He that stands while holding you
Who keeps you upright
Ready for each and every fight
Your might is not your own
Though time and time you say you are grown
But to the Father, his children we will always be

Terry L. Ware, Sr.

Love in a Moment

In a blink of an eye I noticed you
Noticed your smile
It was as if through your eyes I could see you
Your beauty far beyond the outside that others see
I could see you
The most divine woman that I've ever seen
Somehow I swear your heart smiled at me
Maybe that's why away I just couldn't look
For my attention you captured with just one look
You took me by my mind
Gave me just a glimpse of what I would have if you were mine
See
It wasn't that I knew you for years
But
Within just a simple moment
Your heart showed me every tear
Every pain it had to endure
That was unbearable
Yet
I couldn't look away
For if I turned
You may have walked away
So my focus intact
And
At the very end of that moment
I knew just what you needed
Simply because I paid attention
That moment of love
In which I found you

It's Ok

You came into this world as innocent as can be

No flaws, no worries, just a beautiful smile for everyone to see

You grew older and with each day you became stronger

It wasn't hard to see the extravagance in your life, the kindness, the unselfishness, your willingness to always be there

As many looked at you, they admired you, even wanted to be just like you… you were considered a hero, many a justification for living everyday

No matter what it was you were always involved, no matter what circumstance, you would always pull through

There wasn't a day that went by that I didn't see you smile, as if nothing in your life was wrong and everything was fine

No hand outs would you ever take, instead you said someone else would need it more than you

On that very sad day we all had tears in our eyes, but in my ear I heard your voice as it whispered and said "Everyone dies."

So let not this day be a sad day, or even a day to mourn

Rejoice with me and be happy as I, for I have been called home

Flesh of My Flesh, Bone of My Bone

Flesh of my flesh
Bone of my bone
For the cause of righteousness
Even He was stoned

Flesh of my flesh
Bone of my bone
Whenever I am in need
He has proved He is the one

Flesh of my flesh
Bone of my bone
Everything He completes
And nothing is ever left undone

Flesh of my flesh
Bone of my bone
He loved us so much
For our sins He gave up his Son

Flesh of my flesh
Bone of my bone
No matter what
I'm determined to see Him
I'm determined to make it home

Hypothetically Speaking

Hypothetically speaking

If I told you that next to God you are all I need, would you believe me

Hypothetically speaking

If I told you that you meant the world to me, in a sense would you become my world

Hypothetically speaking

If I told you that the rib God took from my side He placed it in you, would you feel it to be true

Hypothetically speaking

If I told you that from you I know I could learn so much, would you be up to the task of teaching me

Hypothetically speaking

If I told you that your love I breathed, and to you my heart have cleaved

Would you love me unconditionally and handle my heart with care

Hypothetically speaking

If I told you that your smile brightens my day, would you continue to smile each and every day

Terry L. Ware, Sr.

Hypothetically speaking

If I told you that for an eternity with you is where I desire to be, would you trust me enough to be with me for an eternity

Hypothetically speaking

If I told you that I love you, would you in return love me and our love be unconditional

Hypothetically speaking

I Apologize

It seems all has gone wrong and the fault points at me

I apologize

I never listened to you

I never took the time out to understand you

I apologize

I was always out with the fellas

I never took time out for you

I guess I figured you would always be there

I apologize

Looking back, I never took the time out to let you know you were special

I never said I love you, only would I reply "me too"

I apologize

I looked you directly in your eyes

Knowing everything that came out my mouth was lies

I could see the hurt in your eyes

Yet went on my way

I apologize

Terry L. Ware, Sr.

I rejected you time and time again

And never once realized

Realized that I had a true woman

A woman that would've had my back no matter what

I apologize

I failed at one of the most important things in life

Love

Now I sit here knowing you will never come home to me

I sit here alone with my heart whole but feeling torn

And all I can say is

I apologize

Sometimes when you finally reach that point of apology, it is just too late

I Dreamed As I Walked

I dreamed as I walked

I walked as I dreamed

While keeping a steady line and pace

Never to turn back on those things that I once faced

Distressed from those things, many said a disgrace

But keeping my head high, those things I now lace

Lace with faith to know those things are taking me to a better place

So as I continue to walk, I'll continue to dream

For if I ever stop, I'll be amongst those past things

For if I ever stop, my dream will never be a reality

Terry L. Ware, Sr.

Advice Un-trusted

Now things are turned around and you believe, as I once did. I guess He wanted to see if you believed all the things you said.

It seems you did not, and matters, like I, you took in your own hands. His hand is stretched out to you like it was to me, but like me you are too blind to see.

Those words you once spoke were only words to pass the time, because you really didn't believe all those burdens were mine.

But those words you spoke somehow reached into my mind. And though I didn't want to hear them, in my soul is where they would call home.

You spoke words of wisdom even when I had a match of negativity in my life to defend, but little did I know my negativity would get under your skin.

But could it really be? You're words you gave all to me, and now you have none to lean on.

Naw, don't make that excuse. When we have nothing to lean on, He is always there to carry us on.

Remember the footprints and how He carries us through. The thing is, too many think that it is what we do that takes us through.

So please remember the advice that you give may be the advice that you will one day need. But the question is can this advice you trust, and your life will it lead???

All of Me

You've been through a lot of false love
Many heart breaks and promises left you feeling all hope was gone
Tears shed from pain that filled your mind
Unable to release for the thought of things will be different this time
Head clouded with thoughts that, maybe in a woman, you would find peace
Giving up on men is what you promised because of excuses that left your heart demolished
A small chance is all I ask, for the love I have for you will have your feelings once again unmasked
To hurt you would be as my heart losing beats
Torn from within never to breathe again
Never to say those things you've heard in past times
But to do those things you've always desired that have never left your mind
In your life I place my heart, to the end from the start
Trust takes time, and in time I will prove that I can be trusted with your heart
When situations arise, when hard times come, my promise to you is to never take flight
By your side is where I will always stand
Never saying I love you until I have proven that I am your man
Place your hand in mine and let our hearts join as one
For this journey has just begun, and my job of loving you will never be done

Terry L. Ware, Sr.

A Father's Love

I was ecstatic as I first held you

Ten fingers, ten toes, two ears, two legs, two arms, two feet, two eyes, one head, one mouth, one nose

The feeling that I got that day no one can erase

As you smiled at me, tears fell from my face

As if you knew the love I had for you I would always embrace

And in my arms you knew you would always be safe

I couldn't take my eyes off you like we were the only ones in the room

Words being spoken without the movement of your lips

Yet every word I completely understood

My seed finally has been birthed through the pains and strains within your mother, God blessed you to see earth

I vow to love you through the good, to love you through the bad

To love you through the mistakes you make

To love you through my rules at times which you will break

Love's Recipe

I promise to be your example of what many fail to be, a real man

To raise you the best I can, to prepare you for the ups and downs of life

You are my seed, my life, my dream

Everything I do is for your life, and to better your life I will go through the most extreme

As long as I breathe, I will love you with the love from my heart

For that is where a father's love starts

Terry L. Ware, Sr.

As I Look In the Sky

I see endless possibilities to all my hopes and dreams

As I look in the sky

I see you and me doing a many of great things

As I look in the sky

I see all your fears, all your disappointments, but most of all I see the love you need

As I look in the sky

I see no limit to what I would do for you, because you are my dream come true

As I look in the sky

I yearn for your soul, because your soul with mine would make this seem like a perfect world

As I look in the sky

With every beat my heart pumps, it says I love you, I love you, I love you because my heart is what you have

As I look in the sky

In your eyes lies my destiny and everything I ever dreamed

Therefore as I look in your eyes I am looking in the sky

How Can I Breathe

What have you done to me… this feeling that lies within me I simply can't explain

Sitting all alone at times… it's like the thought of you drives the blood through my veins

My eyes close and I picture you next to me… smiling that beautiful smile letting me know that everything will be fine

The funny thing is we never spend time together… only conversations on the phone time to time

Yet I yearn to hear your voice… because that is what keeps me

Keeps me moving day to day… knowing that without you life would be fatal

I ask myself at times how did I get here… how did I allow myself to fall for you in such a short period

It gets harder and harder every day… knowing that I yearn to but can't see you face to face

Many would say that I was crazy and possibly insane… but little do they know that my sanity lies within you

How could one person make another feel this way…

Terry L. Ware, Sr.

How can a love be so strong within only a matter of days

My head pounds and pounds… my blood pressure seems to rise, because with you is where I want to be

But my situation has me tangled… and until I am untangled as long as you are there, I will continue to breathe

Love's Recipe

How Did I Get Here ~ Love

Tangled up in the bliss of your love

I often wonder if this is right or possibly wrong

But how could a love of this stature be completely wrong

When the way that I feel often has my mind gone

Gone to a place where I wish to never return

Gone to a place where only you and I exist

Every thought of you brings a peaceful yet exuberant feeling

A feeling that I try to ignore day in and day out but I am left with no words to explain

Being with you I feel feelings I have never felt

Being with you I say things I would not have normally dealt

You are an inspiration to my life a comforter to my strife

But yet I am wondering how has this come about

I am stuck in a world where the walls seem to constantly enclose on me

Where the pain runs through my veins side by side with my blood

See where I am now my soul seems to close with every breath

But just the thought of you seems to bring my soul to life

It's as if you are my life support though I am not connected to you

It's as if I am connected to the wrong power source and connected to you is where I belong

I ask myself where do I go from here, how do I cope with just being verses being just with you

How do I control these feelings without hurting from losing my serenity

How can I not stay wondering what life would be like with you?

How Did I Get Here ~ Life

How did I get here, every breath I breathe is pain!

How did I get here, staring in the sky begging please stop the rain!

How did I get here, troubles fill my life like a flowing river, each day I pray for a drought so it would just stop!

How did I get here, I feel out of control like a freight train that has to crash before it stops!

How did I get here, the leakage of my brain comes from memory loss trying to find myself at any cost!

How did I get here, seems like I'm lying on a curb with my head bashed in, somebody please stop the pain and suffering!

How did I get here, at times standing in a room filled of voices yet I can't hear one because of bad choices!

How did I get here, hands filled with dirt, so much so that nothing can wash it away, not bleach, not even the strongest soap!

How did I get here, playing in a game that never stops, shooting silent guns with no pop!

How did I get here, swimming in a pool with no water yet drowning with every stroke!

Terry L. Ware, Sr.

How did I get here, with every bite I take the food I consume seems to leave me choked!

How did I get here, seems like I'm flying at times though my feet never leave the ground!

How did I get here, bright lights shine in my face yet I can't tell night from day!

How did I get here, feels like I'm being bet on with no luck like a brotha whose winning streak has been struck!

How did I get here, when did my determination for success become fear!

How did I get here is not the question but rather how do I get from here!

I'm Dreaming

U and me, could this be

I must be dreaming

The smile of an angel, shining upon me

I must be dreaming

Thought of this moment all of my life

I must be dreaming

The essence of your beauty from the inside I see

I must be dreaming

The connection from the start, you stole my heart

I must be dreaming

Your style, your swag, to the very way you wear your hair

I must be dreaming

Your mind intensity enhances the style of your conversation

Responding one to another with no hesitation

I must be dreaming

Terry L. Ware, Sr.

Your sex appeal has nothing to do with your body, but everything to do with your soul

With every word you speak, the attention of my mind you hold

I must be dreaming

Never have I read, in books it's never been told, the consolation of knowing my soul connects to yours

I must be dreaming

Nothing smoother than the vibe that flows between you and I

Nothing bigger than Christ Jesus but the thought of you makes me sigh

I must be dreaming

The fire from your eyes burns away the negatives from my past

To gaze into those eyes it's as if I lose control

I must be dreaming

Your physical touch is unknown, but the touch from your soul deep within warms my soul

I must be dreaming

If waking up means not having you than let me dream

If Not Me Then Who

I created you from head to toe
All things about you I know
From the pain through life you will feel
Even down to your every meal
Your insides
Yeah, that's by My design
So to you I say
It's not what or how you feel
It's all about those issues, how you deal
Will you run or face them head on
Please know that within you I desire to call home
But because of your insecurities
I'll leave My Grace to surround you
See it doesn't matter what you've done right
Or even what you've done wrong
I'm simply desiring to guide you all the way back home
Now one thing is for sure
At times in life it will feel as though you just can't endure
And it's at those times My strength in you I began to pour
 I created you from head to toe
Your love, your trust
If not in Me than who?

I Wish

I wish life was simple and plain, then maybe it would be easy to breathe again

I wish those cares I have for you were empty, that way it would be easy to walk away

I wish here I never made my home, than I wouldn't dream of what it would be like to be gone

I wish tears were made of stone, that way they would be hard to cry

I wish my alone time wasn't filled with thoughts of you, then maybe I would have time for me

I wish I didn't worry and pray for a better day, then maybe this pain would somehow fade away

I wish I didn't feel the love I feel for you, that way I wouldn't have to wish at all

Love's Recipe

I Was Distracted For a Brief Moment

So everything that seemed
Deemed to be true
Yet I was blind to the fact I was losing me
Indulging in something I knew could never be
Yet the fool is what I seemed to be
It was true I had a thing for you
The mirage you presented said you had a thing for me
Hmmm please
I was trying to drink from an empty pond
From brokenness I was trying to build a bond
I can't lie
It never felt right
In fact the more I tried the more I lied
Myself
That's what I denied
Make believe can be a dangerous thing
On the most impossible
If you're not careful
You'll lean
Just before the fall
My balance was gripped
I stood tall
Otherwise
How could I walk away!
For just a brief moment
I was trapped in my own time
Until I regained consciousness
And began to use my mind!

Terry L. Ware, Sr.

You Raped Me

You have stripped me of something that I once held very valuable

I never did anything to deserve this. I never once gave you the impression of something that wasn't. What is was suppose to be

I never dressed sexy around you. I never wore any make up around you, to once give you the impression that I might seem interested

Why? Why me, why would you want to put this on me… why after I told you time and time again how much I hated to even imagine this feeling

I thought I could trust in you. I thought that I would always have you around as my good friend, my best friend!

But all the time you had other things in mind. All the time you had a plan, you allowed me to express myself to the point until I became… well, until I let my guard down

I only did it because you listened to me. I thought you understood, I thought you were there for me, and that… that is why I felt safe around you. THAT is why I always wanted to be around you

I never would have imagined you, you of all people, would put this on me

But I guess you saw something in me that I just couldn't hide. You saw the real me inside, and that must be why you raped me!!!

Love's Recipe

Raped away my pride because I was too hard hearted to see the love that you tried to show me, the passion that burned in your eyes every time you would be next to me

I should have known the calls that were just because, were because you really cared and were trying to reach out your hand. But still I didn't understand so I pushed your hand away, and within myself told me that I only needed you as a friend

Because as a friend I wouldn't have to commit to you. I would never have to say "I am in love with you" I could love you to an extent, as a friend....

But instead you raped me, raped me of my self pride, my unwillingness to love, my determination to be alone, my desperation to not care

You raped me, but yet I'm not mad. I am filled with this feeling on the inside that I just can't explain and I can't ignore

Every time I see you I feel as if my life depends on your soul to breathe, as if you're smile was my sunshine and without it I could not find my way

You raped me in a way that has my mind clear, my love flowing freely without fear, and my heart beating without the pain that it once felt

You raped me, took all fear away, and filled my life with the love I thought I could never give

You made me love you when it seemed there was no hope and I know my life would not have ever been this way if you hadn't saved me...

Terry L. Ware, Sr.

Circular Emotions

Sitting patiently while watching

Hearing but not speaking

Gazed in a daze feeling lost in time

Not wanting much, just a peace of mind

Clouded by fear, thoughts seeming unclear

Will I ever find my way through these restless tears

Filling my life, this stress that causes pain

Day to day I struggle to pray

Drinking from the cup of empty happiness

While stuffing my face with daily disgrace

Feeling in this life, I've been misplaced

Looking for rest while traveling from place to place

Only to find within each place thorns are laced

Deep within my heart love you will find

Deep within my heart love hides

My desires fill my soul and wishes to be out poured

Yet my desires like clutter have remained horded

Contact

As you stood there, every word from your lips grasped my attention
Intensely awaiting the next word after the next
Gazed upon the very existence that you stood in
My eyes never left yours
With each response it seemed they were more than just words
They were the stitch to my wounds
A long awaited conversation
Intriguing and so intensely satisfying
My mind
Was in tune to your mind
As you spoke every line
Though we conversed back and forth
Your heart said to mine
It was time
With every laugh you slowly became mine
Nothing sexual
Just the way our souls intertwined
The very first day we met
Was the very first day of us!

Terry L. Ware, Sr.

Definition of a Man

Standing tall regardless of his size
Ready and willing through each situation, he will always rise
Never setting his self above anyone else
Knowing that throughout his life he hasn't been the best
Recognizing that in everyone there lies faults
But knows how to cipher through them and if need be, beside them he can walk
He knows his past and what could have been
Strives to stay on the right track, but knows a part of him will always be some type of sin
Doesn't brag on his capabilities, rather knows himself and is confident of his capabilities
A real man stands up to what a woman needs
Without feeling the need to always plant his seed
He knows that in every woman lies a different definition
And therefore takes his time to learn her composition
He knows that through her desires is how he must get inside of her
And thus makes her desires a part of him so that he can somewhat see inside of her

Love's Recipe

He realizes that this is not a man's world, rather God's world and it will take His guidance to lead his home
A man knows that time spent equals knowledge known
And therefore only worries and stays at his own home
He sees life in a different mantle than he once did
And knows God's word is right, therefore putting away the old kid
He knows that excuses are only made to try and cover the laziness of life
Weaving through the obstacles taking credit for his faults and at the same time striving to learn with all his might
A real man is strong in mind and heart, thus able to win any fight
Never staying down for the count, but rather in every situation a lesson learned for improvement will count

Terry L. Ware, Sr.

From My Heart to Yours

Connected

Soul to soul

Mind to mind

Thought to thought

Hand in hand through life non stop

Round in circles, our time will come

Thorns and blisters sometime will be the outcome

Giving up will never be an option

Approaching each situation with serious caution

Love runs deep

Not just between the sheets

Only for one night, naw I'm talking a lifetime

For me and you, I'll be yours and you'll be mine

With every breath I breathe

I promise you'll always be my sunshine

Love's Recipe

I'm In Search of but I'm Not Looking

I'm in search of a soul mate, not just someone to date

I'm in search of that one that can truly love and never hate

I'm in search of one that can hold the key to my heart

That can love me even though at times I miss the mark

I'm in search of my destiny, everything I've ever dreamed

I'm in search of so many things

But it seems these things are not in search of me

I'm in search of the realism that a woman holds

And not the fake-ism that she consoles

I'm in search of real brotherly love and not the love that doesn't fit like an old glove

I'm in search of who I can be and not who I used to be

I'm in search of new ways of living and not living the way society thinks I should live

I'm in search of life itself and no longer shall life live me

I'm in search of but I am not looking

For if I search within the love of God and seek Him first He said all these things shall be added unto me

So no longer will I search the earth for life and all that lies within

But I will search after God's heart so He can fill me within

For all that I desire I know He will allow me to find

I Am Not What I Was

Surrounded by pain
Left all alone with nothing to gain
Insanity has become my fame
Walking around smiling yet filled with shame
Lame
Yeah, I know, that's what they say as they open my door
To cope with me means to be doped up like me
Yet
Never realizing the problem that in you lies
I know because I've been there
Sometimes seems as if I'm still there
But
What I have now found keeps me level with my feet on the ground
Has changed my closed mind
Replaced with a peace of mind
Now I don't mind sharing this with you
Hope is not lost
For He paid your cost
That pain you feel is a temporary ill---ness
Drop the ness that leaves the ill
I live long!
Simply because His spirit within me roams

Terry L. Ware, Sr.

I Could, But Why

I could write this poem about a thousand reasons

To blame you for my pain

But why

When that pain has made me

Into a true man!!!

I could

But why???

Love's Recipe

I Got a Jones

With every word you speak, you seduce my mind and send chills down my spine

Never did I imagine being entrapped with such a love that has my thoughts over flowing

My feelings race daily while my heart indulges itself in yours

The refresh-ness of your personality has me so, till all I can do is brag about you

Somehow you find your way into my dreams because everything I dream seems to become reality

Just being held in your arms means more to me than all the money I could ever have

For when I am in your arms, I know this is the safest place I could ever be

I can trust you with my feelings knowing that when I tell you I love you, I'm embraced with that same love

If not more, and not take advantage and use that love against me

Every time we kiss is like the very first time, so special till the point my body shivers with just the thought of kissing you

Terry L. Ware, Sr.

There is no definition to define the feelings that I feel, for these feelings are too much to put into just one word

The bedroom is full of sexual healing, passionate emotions, soul in soul, mind in mind

I would say cloud nine, but there I have been and never have I seen or felt this love that just puts me out of my mind

I can truly say I have found the true definition of love, for there is nothing that you can ask that I will not do

I will never imagine being without you, for just the thought of you not here makes it hard to breathe

This love is so pleasing that it brings to my eyes tears knowing that this jones I have for you is as real as love will ever be

I Never Knew You

I never knew you, but I've always felt you

I never knew you, but if I ever came close to you I would know you

I never knew you, but in life I've always desired you

I never knew you, but my heart has always had love for you

I never knew you, but I swear I would give my all to you

I never knew you, yet my eyes always see you

I never knew you, yet I always breathed you

I never knew you, yet with every thought my life is inspired

I never knew you, so why is it I can't stop thinking of you

I never knew you, so why is it my heart yearns for you

I never knew you, so why is it my life depends on you

I never knew you, but the very essence of you sparks sunshine in my life

I never knew you, but in my dreams it seems as if I converse with you

I never knew you, but how will I know you until I first find me!!!

Terry L. Ware, Sr.

Consequences of Actions

Was it worth the pain that you feel right now

Was it worth the tears that streamed down your face every time I looked at you

Was it worth the depression that caused you headache after headache

Was it worth the trust that you lost in me because of decisions that I made

Was it worth the lies that I filled your mind with because of my inability to be a man

Was it worth the many nights that you stayed up all night waiting to just hear from me that I was alright

Was it worth the slipping and tipping, the ducking and dodging, the mistreatment of your love time and time again

Was it worth the dinners I missed, the holidays I wasn't there, the birthdays that I stood you up

Was it worth the heart break that I caused you, the imperativeness that I tried to place upon you

Was it worth all the true love that I had in you that is now gone

Was it worth losing you all because I couldn't keep my love at home

Love's Recipe

Unconditional

Hidden deep within the soul

From one to another, there to console

Destined to be

Together through life for an eternity

Hurts that blind from time to time

Through it all a love that will always shine

A love that is seasoned

Mending relationships is the agreement

Put to the test time and time again

Destined for growth for there is no end

To get it right all the time is not the key

But

Rather how you learn from each situation you see

Whether in the same state or miles apart

The love for family should remain in our hearts

What I See

As I look within your eyes I become mesmerized for the things I see within

For all the love you have to share, it seems to be held up because of situations that leave you emotionally stressed

It's not hard to see all the qualities that God has placed within you

But for some reason no one takes the time to appreciate the beauty of a queen with a soul that yearns for true love

As the blood flows through your body, the enrichment of your heart is what keeps that beautiful smile shining

So as the sun lights up the sky with your smile dark days seem less and less

The seduction of your eyes tell the story of the woman that you are and of things you will do to make one feel special

Through your eyes I see a real woman, a woman who knows how to handle her business

A woman, not a lil girl, that makes the hardest decision seem simple and plain

Out of all the things that I see within, it is easy to see that the beauty on the inside overflows to the outside which makes you more extravagant than any beauty queen

When I Met You

Stuck in a place of false identity

Living a life looking for gratuity

From one place to the next

Stopping where I thought was best

Only to find out there was no rest

Confused with low self esteem

Traveling this journey with no dreams

Wondering why those things I would do

With no justification and no real proof

Stuck at a crossroad which way do I go

Decisions so hard I'd just rather let go

Is it real can life really be this bad

Or is it just the choices I've made that have left me sad

They say life goes on and we must live

So why am I sitting around waiting for it to end

Terry L. Ware, Sr.

A lot of questions I've had but the answers I've always feared

Till the day I finally took the time to look in the mirror and realized nothing was as it appeared

I looked into those eyes as they stared back

This confidence I see I've always lacked

Something trickled inside while I stood there

For the first time I realized who I was and my life became clear

When It's Your Fault

The pain is unbearable… your mind can't focus on things at hand, when it's your fault

Your body feels like it's on a roller coaster that will never end, when it's your fault

Sleep becomes less and less, and your days get darker and darker, when it's your fault

Your ears hear nothing more than what you want them to hear, when it's your fault

Work becomes unbearable and you can't stand to be there, even more than before, when it's your fault

All your hopes and dreams seem to be shattered and your life seems to come to a pause with every breath you take, when it's your fault

You wonder time to time why you did what you did, knowing it wasn't the right way to go, when it's your fault

Even though you think often about what you did

The fact still remains that you want to blame something or someone else because it just can't be fixed like you think it should be, no matter how much pain you have caused, when it's your fault

When it's all on you

Who else can you blame

Who else to point the finger at once something is done

Once pain sets in, there is always the possibility that it will never be the same, when it's your fault

Love's Recipe

When Love Is Lost

A match seemingly made in heaven

Unbroken bond strong as the toughest levy

Time spent seemed love was meant

Somehow that love was bent

Taken by surprise, never thought without you I would be

Your love is what kept me free

Knowing now the love you have is no longer for me

How I never imagined this day I would see

Moving forward without you, I know not how to do

This love never have I felt

Yet this pain many times by me have been dealt

As the tears pour, my eyes begin to shut

Only your face beneath my lids are tucked

Times thought of that we shared

Times thought of as fear we shared

Terry L. Ware, Sr.

This chance I took, as to you I gave my all

Only to now see my life crumple and fall

Morning is like night, night is like day

As my head rest on my pillow, to my left you no longer lay

Only the scent of your love embraces my senses

Love seems now so senseless

Sleep I feel I must stay, for it is how I runaway

For in my sleep your face I see everyday

This loneliness has changed my world

For in this position I lay as flat as a board

Entrapped within myself enclosed in this room

Praying my Father will take me soon

Don't Wanna

This emotion that I am feeling

Towards love got me leaning

Without a thought to comprehend

I quickly try and find an end

But why?

Why does my mind doubt

The very simple thing I can't do without

It's what I crave

As if this very moment is why my life has been saved

To breath a new air, a different air

To some this may seem unfair

But to me, it's all I've ever dreamed

To be free from pain, free from disappointments

Free from struggles

I know this will never be, but is it possible

Through it all to still be free

This is what I now know you provide me

And without you there would be no me

More and more of you I yearn to know

And because of your love, I refuse to ever let go

Terry L. Ware, Sr.

Emotional Roller Coaster

I've tried my best, done all I can possibly do, now everything that you want to happen is up to you

You say you love me and that you really care, yet when we are apart that love and care is hard to see

Whenever we are together I can sense the love you say you have, and I must admit, it's a wonderful feeling

But tell me how you feel when we are not together, tell me what's really on your mind

Do you think of me as I think of you, does the love you show while with me still burn the same inside

As you look into my eyes and say those three meaningful words, do you still picture my response when you're alone

When we make passionate love and you tell me you never want to hurt me, do you still feel the same when you are with your friends

Could someone possibly be taking my place because I am unable to be there, or is it my imagination in the mirror looking back at me as I stare

My mind flows and wonders every time I say that I trust you, for those words I can't say that I mean, though everyday those words to be true I dream

Love's Recipe

To hurt one more time, I'm sorry, won't happen, I will have to decline

My most inner secrets, my most inner thoughts I wish I could share, but for some strange reason I don't think you would care

Some say I think too much and at times ask too many questions, but I say if my mind stops thinking my stomach would get indigestion

Worrying is what I do, for the hurt has consoled my body for far too long, so on the go my mind will remain, until that day you can take the pain away

Dry my eyes, and empty my heart filled with sorrow, only then will my mind consume what you say, and my throat shall swallow the truth as it is told to me

For now my mind will wonder and my heart fill with sorrow, and on my knees is where I will stay praying for a better tomorrow

Terry L. Ware, Sr.

Finally In Love

Sitting here feeling the many emotions of what I feel and where it has brought me

I would have never imagined it would be this way, the things I have inside of me

Tell me is this what it's all about? Does bad really come from caring and allow me to have doubt

It feels real, my mind tells me it's real, my soul even yearns for it…and yet sometimes I feel low as if I was deep in a pit

It can't be, that's not what it's about. It's suppose to make you feel good at all times and never hurt, uplift your spirits and never make you feel down

But how can I tell? How would I know if I've never been here before

I really don't understand. Some say that I am, some say I might be, this is just too much for me

I can't eat, I can't sleep. She pisses me off with the sound of her grinding teeth

And yet I can't get her off my mind. Whenever I'm not with her it's like I'm lost and only my soul she can find

It's a mystery to me, one I don't think I want to know how it will end. What if this is just not meant to be? What if I fail like all the other times I've given it a try, what if now is not my time

Love's Recipe

It's been a long time coming, I'm just too old now, it just can't happen to me, I missed my turn long ago, I feel I must move on and let this feeling go

Should I, could I, I mean I do love her and can't stand to be without her? She brightens my day by just being there

Naw, there are so many things about her that I don't like, that get on my nerves but yet there are little things, things that don't really matter when I think about it

Why is it so confusing? It's suppose to be simple, you are suppose to know for a fact if this feeling is so

But yet I just can't let go, this feeling has me hooked on wanting to know

Could it be, could this feeling be that of true love??????????????????????????

Terry L. Ware, Sr.

Focus

A refreshing thought entered my mind

At the simple moment I thought I would never find

The compressions of your wanting to fulfill your passions

The desires that turn into your needs

But those needs you never seem to feed

Instead

You focus on lifeless things; you breathe those things that are detrimental to your actual needs

Those passions become lost with every breath and are replaced

With nothing

For nothing is what you have found though you thought it would hold you down

Instead it was as a simple feather blowing in the wind with just a simple breeze

And before you knew it, it was as if it no longer existed

The compression of your wanting to fulfill your passions

Can simply be lost within a mirage

A refreshing thought entered my mind

At the very moment I awoke and began to focus on the needs of my passions

Love's Recipe

From My Heart to Yours

Connected

Soul to soul

Mind to mind

Thought to thought

Hand in hand through life non stop

Round in circles our time will come

Thorns and blisters sometime will be the outcome

Giving up will never be an option

Approaching each situation with serious caution

Love runs deep

Not just between the sheets

Only for one night, naw I'm talking a lifetime

For me and you, I'll be yours and you'll be mine

With every breath I breathe

I promise you'll always be my sunshine

Terry L. Ware, Sr.

Life's Renovation

For the thoughts of love fill my mind

Drowning my soul as I travel through time

Blood clots consume my veins

Arteries blocked by this feeling we call pain

The capacity of my lungs have been shrunken like a bud

No cigarette smoke just the absence of love

My kidneys slowly failing, my intestines are shivering up

From the stones that were thrown have now overflowed my cup

My knees weakened from constantly going in prayer

No one ever told me that life would be this unfair

But live I must before I totally lose touch

Crawling through life with less and less trust

Eyes being deceived from constantly losing my focus to breathe

Love's Recipe

Lips closed tight though my body needs to feed

Continually to dysfunction for multiple false consumptions

No longer do I have time and no longer will I make assumptions

For this time things will be right and the renovation of my life will override the darkness into light

Terry L. Ware, Sr.

Love Letter to Self

One thing you must know

Deep inside for you is where my love flows

No one on earth can please you

No one on earth can feed your soul

No one on earth can push you to your goal

I love you

Sometimes more than life itself

Pushing you past your limits

So you will never be left on the shelf

For you

There are no limits past my limits because they're endless

Restless to show you love

I'll never grow weary

Desperately grasping every part of you

Never letting anyone take advantage of you

Because you are a part of me

And I am a part of you

Constantly growing

Constantly learning more and more

Just a love letter to self to never forget my worth!

Love's Recipe

Love

What is love? Some say it's just a four letter word
Some even say it's absurd
Some say they've heard it all, it doesn't exist like an invisible wall
Could it be it doesn't exist because the meaning to you is unknown
Could it be it doesn't exist because it's what you've never really shown
Love comes and sometimes seems to go
But only because your feelings seemed to have froze
Love is in the air and at times seems to be unfair
It never goes it never leaves because it's something we all need
You say you will never love again
But it's funny when a child is born, love is reborn again
Love starts within, without it life's disappointments couldn't mend

Love's Promise

Overlooking your imperfections

Knowing that you are one of God's greatest creations

Your glow that shows who you truly are

Makes me know I must handle your heart with care

As fragile as can be yet strong in mind is what draws me

Your love is stable as a house built on a strong foundation

To know more of you, to know what lies deep within you, I proceed with no hesitation

My destination to know you through your heart, mind, body and soul

By giving you my all, never hurting you, but will always be there to catch you when you fall

Console in me those things that no one knows

Trust in me… allow me to touch you deep within your soul

Mind stimulation, intellectual conversation, makes for a life filled with togetherness and dedication

As we flow through life slowly enjoying every single moment

To always make you smile and never make you cry

This is my promise for the rest of our lives to always have you on a sensual high

Life and Love

LIFE is given to you by your mother and father

LOVE is what we give back to them for doing so

Life is what we live day to day

Love is what we fear will take our life away

Life is full of disappointments and things that don't go our way

Love is what we are scared will become one, thus we steer far away

Life is full of choices that we must make everyday

Love is what we all want to feel but somehow just can't say

Life we live to die and hope to one day see God's face

Love is what some will never give Him though He gave us all His Grace

Life you may say is hard and unfair, but just remember unlike life, love will always be here

Terry L. Ware, Sr.

Little Feelings of Love

Looking into your eyes I see all that I need to know - - I am in love

The way you touch me gently and moan my name softly, lets me know how deeply you feel me- - I am in love

When you look at me with that sparkle in your eye while telling me you love me, makes me feel like the most special person in the world- - I am in love

The way your petite curves flow while next to me whether in bed or walking down the street, ohhhh…what a perfect fit - - I am in love

How I yearn to be with you every hour of the day and every second of a minute- - I am in love

When talking to your friends mentioning the qualities I posses as a man, bragging, yeah, letting them know how happy you are- - I am in love

Every minute without you, every second you are gone, short breaths I take because without you I'd be gone- - I am in love

Every night on my knees thanking God for these days, because these days is what I would always plead- - I am in love

Love's Recipe

To never have met you, to never have felt your touch, to never have known your weakness and strengths, would be like I never was here- - I am in love

Waking up every morning next to you, the taste of your morning breath, the look of your wild hair, or the crust in your eyes I look forward to- - I am in love

You are the missing bone from my body, the spice I needed in my recipe, the anchor to this ship, the missing piece to my puzzle, the joy in my life whenever things turn out bad, my woman you are, your man I am and with you- -I am in love

Terry L. Ware, Sr.

Love or Lust

Sexy, a dime, unimaginative, just a few words to describe you

Looks at first sight can get you caught up and even make you think that your thoughts of a long lasting relationship are true

Inside you ignore for the outside has your eyes in a blur

Dates you go on, time you spend, still doesn't bring your mind to reality

Reality that if you focus too much on the outside, the inside your mind will never reach

The love hidden deep within, you will never know, only the love you felt the night before

You use those words because you never felt what you say you feel now

And this love you say in your mind is no doubt

But how can you truly love, how can you truly know the difference unless you first indulge into the inside

For on the inside lies hidden the things that are needed to know, the things that make someone's life flow

On the outside, a pepper seems to be nice and smooth

Love's Recipe

But once on the inside you find and feel all its grooves

You find the pain that it causes, and sometimes the tears that it brings

We often see mirages as beautiful as they are but in the end they fade away and we're left with nothing

We tend to sell ourselves short because we stop before we reach the finish line

We say we love someone when we really love the essence of their beauty- the outside

The kindness of their smile, or the softness of their touch

When their heart, their mind, and their soul is what we should clutch

Love for better or worse, through thick and thin, until the end

Lust for the one time feeling with no intention

Love or lust you must first determine for the prevention of a life time hurt

Terry L. Ware, Sr.

It's Time

Often times we sit and ask the question
Why
Why pain
Why suffering
Why at times we feel more loss
Than gain
Question
Have you ever stopped to look at you?

Brothers
The game got you feeling big
The thug in you
Tells you
By many you are feared
And somehow the ladies
Love you for that fear
But have you ever stopped to think
Maybe you aren't the player
See I've played the game
Naw wait
In reality the game played me
Had me thinking I had it going on
When really I had no where to call home
Had plenty of women
Yet
Not one woman!
Oh how thankful I am for God's Grace
The thug in you tells you that you're the man
The ladies love you because that sense of protection
Yet

Love's Recipe

What they fail to understand
It's like a sale
That last for a limited time
Robbing, killing, selling dope
Whatever your poison
It's giving you less and less hope
And to your seeds
You're selling that same hope
When will we stand up
When will we realize that without us
How can our boys learn to be men
How can they learn what it means to be
A family man
Not a lady's man
It's time they learned the real definition
Of man

Sisters
Yeah
You fly
In your Pravda, Dolce & Cabaña
Vera Wang, Juicy Couture
Donna Karin, Marc Jacobs
Yet
What does it say
With your breasts overflowing your tops
While your bottoms so tight
There's no air left to breathe
Yeah, I know
It's your money
It's the way you like to dress
Very true, and I dare not condemn you
But

Terry L. Ware, Sr.

I'll give you something to think about
See it's not about the way you dress
Rather the message that is sent
You feel the need to show all your curves
That's what attracts the players, thugs and duds
Yet
You say you want a real man
First learn the definition of a real wo-man!
Let your sexiness show through your brain
Then, maybe then
You will feel less and less pain
It's like studying to be a doctor
But using law material
No matter how you swing it
You will miss every time
I'm simply just saying
It's time
Stop being passed from man to man
In that the saddest thing is
They're not the ones doing the passing
It's you
You're searching for gold
While digging through bronze
Though the colors are similar
It's the shine that sets them apart

I dare not judge anyone
Or call myself better than you
I'm just breaking down the simplicities
Of a fool
The fool I once was
And still climbing away from…
You're special

Love's Recipe

You have purpose
There is a destiny just for you
God gave his Son so we didn't have to play the fool
Yet
We find ourselves a comfort in the lining of a fool
A fool is simply one who knows better
But chooses the other, for the satisfaction of being wanted
Un-adulterated passiveness
Causes those things we know we want
Yeah, we walk on by
Look ourselves in the mirror
And lie to our own eyes
This is a wakeup call
For which some of you will hit snooze
Looking for that little extra rest
Amongst the trickery of your mess
But then
There are those that think like me
When that sound goes off
They will awake and know
It's time

Terry L. Ware, Sr.

Mirage

What is love?
Some say it's only a four letter word
In fact they even compare it to the beauty of a dove
A bird that shines within itself
Captivated from others until the time comes of its use
Then it soars through the air as free as can be
Only to disappear in the wind never again to be seen
Representation of love to most, this is the meaning
Only pulling it out to use it to your benefit yet never comprehending the true meaning
Once it's used, now you've gotten what you want
It disappears in the wind never again to be seen
Left one feeling empty with thoughts of what if
While you've moved on looking for another prey
Never realizing the hurt in which you leave behind
Not only the hurt but a piece of yourself as well each time
Standing for nothing, falling with time, never stopping to once use your mind
The constant cycle of never changing got you thinking that to everyone a gift you are
They see what you can't see, a human blinded by fantasy
Not even worthy to be called a man or woman, because they just can't see
I pray you open your eyes, expand your mind, become how God has created you to be
For if not, only grains of dirt will be the last thing others see

Loving Is Not Being in Love

Don't tell me you are in love with me
When you only love me

You say you are in love with me
    but you refuse to open up to me
You say you are in love with me
    yet you always lie to me
You say you are in love with me
    but you can't accept me for me
You say you are in love with me
    yet you can't help me when I need you
You say you are in love with me
    but I never feel love when we make love
You say you are in love with me
    yet you never take time to listen to me
You say you are in love with me
    but you'd rather be out with your friends
You say you are in love with me
    yet you hardly spend time with me
You say you are in love with me
    but never say I love you
You say you are in love with me
    yet you continue to do everything I tell you
    to …aggravate me
You say you are in love with me
    but not like I am in love with you

Find out what being in love is all about before you steal someone's heart with those magical words. And remember loving is not being in love.

Terry L. Ware, Sr.

Moving Forward

Traveling through life trying to find my way

Through tough situations, sometimes pain made it hard to make it through the day

Problems with friends, family, and sometimes within

Doing right seems to have stress that follows, why can't I be like the rest and not care

Why can't I feel little about what others think

How come in life there is so much pressure, in this world how will I ever measure

Thoughts after thoughts race through my mind, from one grade to the next, from one situation to the next, peace will I ever find

I prayed and prayed and finally an answer came down from above

"I didn't make you like the rest, instead for you I have only the best. So take your time, let me ease your mind, in time you will find, what I have in store for you."

Now I know the world will always have obstacles, and people that don't want me to succeed

But one thing is for sure, God has already planted my seed

So into this new world as I enter, never alone or shall I ever fear, because no matter what lies ahead my Father will always be near

My Angel

It's like you never left

The essence of your smell

Every day I inhale

Thoughts of you penetrating my mind

With those simple words

Of

"Everything will be just fine"

I know I got to move on

But why

Why did He choose you

Instead of I

I'd give anything just to hold you again

You were more than my lover

You were my closet friend

There was never an end

Because your love was straight from the heart

Never a thought

Whether you would gain in return

Never wondered when it would be your turn

You always said

In giving

Terry L. Ware, Sr.

That was your turn

Now I'm sitting here

With feelings of love

Not knowing which way to turn

Yet remembering

You would always say

No matter what

Life goes on

But see that's just the thing

This love I have for you

Will forever go on

I learned so much

Through the connection of you

Now I just have to learn

How to make it without you!!!!

Love's Recipe

My Soul Bleeds

This was not suppose to happen

How did it come to this

This time was suppose to be right

This time I just knew would be different

But instead I find myself troubled

Troubled by my inner feelings

The things that I feel boggle my mind

Moves deep within my soul trying to weigh me down

My heart pumps harder and harder till my veins start to show

I must try to breathe before my body becomes a freak show

What am I to do, what am I to say

I try harder and harder to focus each day

Yet the more I try, seems the more pain I feel

I've felt pain before, actually, plenty of times

But somehow this pain here, I truly thought would never be mine

Terry L. Ware, Sr.

Things I try and do seem not to be enough

Sometimes it gets hard to see how I will make it on this earth

I cry and I cry and I cry

So much until I feel this pain in my eyes

I'm not understanding, I just can't comprehend

I thought she would be my world, my lover, my truest friend

Instead it seems she understands not

And even more devastating, my feelings she takes light

But now the time has come for me to make a decision

But my decision I will not make until God himself shows me the way

Because one thing I truly know, this pain will take me to a better day

New World

Entering a new world I know nothing about, interesting things I will find I have no doubt

A little nervous I must admit, but I desire to know more so further is where I go

To the core is where I'm trying to get, but I'll stop here for conversation so you I can get to know

A little here, a little there, bits and pieces of things I pick up and thus more of me I share

With you I shall spend quality time, how else will I find out what lies inside

I shall explore every inch of you to know your weak and strong points, nothing I will ignore

To listen as your wind blows, just so I don't miss anything you might want me to know

When it rains I feel your pain, when the storms arise I am there to dry your eyes

No one or nothing can keep me from becoming one with this world, for I am determined to defend it at any given cost for this world I will make sacrifices so the sun will always shine

Terry L. Ware, Sr.

This will be my world, and the core I shall reach, for my love is too deep, and determination is too divine, so right now I want to let you know, that in time your love I shall find

But for now this world I shall explore, all of the frustrations, I will shut the door, disappointments will be no more

These are the promises I make unto this world, because this world will one day be one with me

No Goodbyes

I thought I'd say goodbye
Yet no words came to mind
I thought I'd try it in another way
Yet no way I found
I began to think of all the good times
Wait
That would require them to be implanted on the mind
So I reached down further
Surely there would be something I'd find
Only emptiness clutches my hand
As if I was trying to find rocks in rockless sand
The picture was being painted
Yet I failed to see it clear
Time and time again
I made up my own thoughts
In order to explain the pain
I even told myself maybe, just maybe
This was a part of the plan
Somehow I decided to finally open my mind
That's when the clearest thought suddenly shined
How can one say goodbye
When they never said hello
Therefore, I simply just walked away!!!

Terry L. Ware, Sr.

My Children

Now I lay Me down to sleep

I promise to watch over My children while they sleep

And if one should past before they wake

I only ask their soul will be ready for Me to take

For all my children I truly love

No matter the shape, form, or size

Important are all their lives

Though at times it seems some ignore Me

I hold true to My word because of the love I see within

No matter how many try to hide it deep inside

I know it's there because all are My design

Many of my little ones I call to Me

Oh how such a shame when others speak down of them when they speak of Me

Love's Recipe

Out of the schools have they taken Me

Trying to completely wash away My name

Oh how thankful am I for my children that are not ashamed

My love for all will never change

But oh what a shame if in the book of life lies not your name

Terry L. Ware, Sr.

My God

You took me under your wing and never let me go

You showed me what love was, now I can share with everyone what I know

You never let me down, nor left me all alone

Your humble place, one day I will call home

No matter what I do, I can always count on You

I never have to worry, because You will always be true

To everyone I say, believe, because He is real, too many times has He proven Himself to me, and deep down in my heart is where my God will always live

No Regrets

Out of everything I have been through I say thank you

Thank you to all who have caused me pain

For the pain I have felt in the past, today has made me have a better plan

Those times when I thought I couldn't I did, and those times I wanted to die, I lived

Those times you used me for only things that benefited you was because I allowed you to

Not because you had so much game or because I clung to your every word

But because I yearned for love and in reality I had no idea of love

For the times I was locked up with the fear of never being who God created me to be

For the times I cried all night from being blinded without sight to see that this situation I just should not be in

The times that it seemed I just couldn't get it right, like everything I did failed and everything I dreamed faded out of sight

For the times I turned my back on those that loved me as if they were strangers unknown to me

Terry L. Ware, Sr.

For the moves I made with no direction, with no hesitation, clouded with frustration

Things that I thought in my mind to wish wrong to others, to wish that hurt would fall upon them

I only wanted them to feel what I felt to know the pains that ran through each and every limb

Where was my blood for I could hardly move at times, it seemed as if pain only flowed through my veins

But no regrets do I have, for how can I help others not to feel what I felt, to see the things that I've seen

To understand those things that I never had a clue, to feel love I never felt

How can I teach you not to be what was me if I regretted the things that can now help you

For all that I have ever went through has allowed me to be who I am today

So regrets are not an option, for without those disappointments I might not have made it where I am today

Our Day

This day will be the first day that we are as one

This day will mark the first day of the rest of our lives

This day unto us will be a very memorable day that no man can take from us

This day I will vow to love and cherish you through thick and thin, for better or worse for the rest of our lives

This day we will look in each other's eyes and say those magical words of "I do"

This day rings will be placed on each other's fingers symbolizing our commitment to each other in which no man can destroy

On this day as our lips gently bind together and our hearts collide as one this will spark the beginning of our marriage for an eternity to come.

This is Our Day

Terry L. Ware, Sr.

Overdosed

Separated from what had my mind tangled, free from everything else

Every moment spent with you I seemed to find myself

Never a dull minute, my soul on high always seemed to be

No worries, I never had to pretend, I could always be me

Now how do I cope with you not here

Losing my mind, my will to live, never being with you again I now fear

Waking up late at night my sheets soaked from sweat of me thinking of you

Making it through the day becomes harder and harder

Tweaking from not having you beside me, feening for that love we once shared

My heart can't take it, my mind seems to lose focus

I need to hold you, feel your touch just one more time

Many say for you I have it bad, they've never seen me this way

Love's Recipe

How is it without you life just seems so sad, so empty, like I've lost everything I've had

I find myself short of breath, I can feel my life slipping away

Straps around my wrist, voices all around as I try to find strength to breathe

So cold I feel, never thought like this I would leave, but like this is truly a dream

For your love lies deep within me, as I slip away know this is the happiest I've ever been

Overdosed on your love!!!!!

Terry L. Ware, Sr.

Quiet Storm

It began all of a sudden
As if my life was undone
With the undoing of one button
There wasn't a lot of noise
Things around me seemed the same
But there was this feeling on the inside
All of me it seemed to drain
Everyone around me noticed nothing
They even said a smile I seemed to always have
But deep inside it was as if dark was my path
One situation to the next
Only seemed to compare
To that of a short breath
It was as if I was moving with no movement
And only half of answers I would get
As if He was leaving me hints
Never too caught up in these emotions
My life flowed like sounds of the ocean
It was scary yet satisfying
Never overwhelming
Like a clear sky
Everything I seemed to pass by
Simply put
Resting in His arms
Favored by Grace
This storm was at a steady pace
Never did I have time to see it
Never allowed to ponder on emotions and just sit
I had been carried through some of the most difficult times
Without one scratch
No scars
Now standing in the midst of sunshine

Love's Recipe

Same Ol Love Song

I find myself once again back in the same place

A place where I once said I would never be again

Everything seemed different, everything felt right

But yet somehow instead of going straight, I went right

Right into another twisted situation

From the door all the signs were there

Yet I bypassed them all, because I thought love was in the air

But all along misery and distress is what was in the air

I told myself this time, this time I would be careful

Careful not to put my emotions in front of my decisions

Now once again I'm forced to make a decision, a decision that I should have made before but my emotions blinded me

I feel like I'm stuck in a corner and can't move because I'm in time out

But time out is what I should have taken, instead of rushing in this terrible situation

How do you control your feelings, how do you not fall in love

Terry L. Ware, Sr.

I prayed and I prayed, each and everyday

I guessed what I failed to do was listen after I prayed

Should I now make excuses for what has happened, or should I own up and admit realization is what I was lacking

How could this have happened, how did I allow myself to fall victim

The answer is easy, and the answer I now know

Pray, pray, pray, but don't forget to listen

Not only listen but follow instructions

And you won't have to sing this same ol love song…

Sweet Unity

A new day arises each day I look into your eyes

A true love, not made up, never in disguise

A love I've searched for, many times dreamed, but never imagined it would be a reality

My heart has been touched in so many ways as if your love was versatile with much tranquility

As the sounds of birds cause for sweet relaxation, your love causes my soul to be at ease

Realizing that the perfect peace I have found

Trapped within a box with no reason to smile, your love has restored the sunshine within my smile

As we hold hands our lives become one, our souls encapture one another's
Our dreams now become each other's dreams

More than husband and wife we are jointed friends

Our kids are now a part of both our lives as they become brother and sister they look to us to show how to love

How to be there for one another through the good times and times that will be bad

I love you now, I love you forever, I love you until my heart hurts

I love you for you, for within you have I found the cure to all my hurts

Terry L. Ware, Sr.

Since We Last Spoke

I haven't felt the same and things haven't been in order since we last spoke

My world has been going in circles and I can't seem to shake the feeling of un-realization since we last spoke

Thoughts of things that I could never have imagined have crossed my mind, and not only that, it has made me to feel at ease with myself since we last spoke

The true meaning of what every human being should feel I now know I feel, since we last spoke

I've realized where it is I need to be and what my life was missing all these years, since we last spoke

My hand embraced in yours, just as our hearts in each other's lives, that's what I realized since we last spoke

It's been two hours, 30 minutes, and 15 seconds, and yet as every minute passes I grow deeper in love with you since we last spoke….

Love's Recipe

Stop Lying

You say this and you say that

Yet all your actions are just that, acts

You say sincere is what you are

Like some other people you never play with hearts

Building me up intentions only to tear me down

For some reason you seem to enjoy my frowns

Look me in my eyes and tell me what's on your mind

How can you do that when you are only passing time

Spending time with me day in and day out

But my destination was far from your route

Just thinking of your text

Wishing you were here text

Should have known they were codes for you thinking of the move you would make next

Mind in knots all tangled up

Thought the feelings of love overflowed my cup

Terry L. Ware, Sr.

Naw, just feelings of emotions from what I wanted to feel

While all along my emotions are what you wanted to feel

Just another lame, playing little childish games

Should've kept it real from the start, never know what might just have came

Love's Recipe

The Essence of True Love

As I sit here thinking of your beautiful smile I wonder what it would be like to see that smile everyday

When I wake in the morning, before I leave for work, when I arrive at work to hear your voice telling me you were just calling to say you miss and love me – I can just see that smile

When I come home from work you hug me, and once again you tell me you love me as your smile lights up the room putting all my troubles from work to rest

With me standing there, holding you really feeling loved by the one I care so deeply about

Dinner is not even ready but without a peep I begin to prepare it

This love is so incredible that it seems it could not be real, it must be a dream, I've never felt this way in my life to have a woman to be so real, so true until there is nothing I wouldn't do for her because I know she feels the same

As we sit and watch television after we've eaten, you softly grasp on to my arm and put your head on my shoulder and whisper you love me in that soft, gentle voice of yours

It's time for bed now and as I lay in bed you walk out of the bathroom in your sexy night gown, walking slowly to the bed like a model walks down a run way

Now what happens next is between you and I…….

Not once, not twice, not every now and then, but I'm taking all the time, my day would be this way

Not hearing any complaints about anything, why, because I treat her like a queen and she treats me like a king

I can trust her and I'm not talking about any pretend trust to make me feel good about myself, I'm talking about real genuine trust where there's no need to worry because not only does she tell me how much she cares, she shows it 100%

To be able to love someone in that manner and have them show that same love in return is something so special that for something to make you upset wouldn't matter because only the thought of that love would show up and you wouldn't even want to think about the situation

Some may say "well how you know it's not a front, how you know she's not out there with someone else, and is putting on a front to throw you off" I say to them my heart tells me so

Will this love actually ever come about, some say it's just a fairytale and it only happens in the movies, but I say it exists and it takes two to accomplish...

"How can two hearts truly come together, unless they first collide?"

Suicide Love

I'm tired, I'm beat, I can't focus for losing sleep

Nothing seems to add up anymore as if I'm stuck behind a trap door

Thoughts hidden deep within, the more I hide the more they divide

Craziness surrounds me, I'm seeing things I should not be

Insane I often feel as this love for you pounds me like a drill

How do I let go of feelings filled with emotions

Day to day feeling as if my life were filled with demotions

I can't take it, it seems so easy to just let it all go

But in return what will I receive, will the same come through my door

What do I have to lose, after all it's my decision to choose

And if I don't I'll ask the question, to stay, am I a fool

Many before me have been very successful, quite often left known as an intellectual

I'm all in, no more time for guessing, if I fail at least there will be a lesson

If I succeed I'll count it as a blessing

So on with this mission I have chosen to go

No stops on the way, for finding your love, my soul I must sow

The Pain I Feel

This pain runs deep

As memories of you I keep

Hidden deep within

I treasured you as a friend

You were taken from this world

From me far too soon

As I looked in your eyes for the last time

I couldn't help the tears I cried

Lying I would be if I said my tears were of joy

For they were tears that you would no longer be a part of my world

Standing there just looking at your face

I prayed and wished I was in your place

I was blessed to call you friend

I still wonder to this day why your life had to come to an end

My mind is filled with the times we laughed and sometimes cried

Terry L. Ware, Sr.

Lonely I feel, grieved I feel, as I stand alone crying with you no longer by my side

Can someone tell me why, why couldn't He just give you one more chance

I swear I would have giving my life to give you that chance

I miss you dearly, I miss you so much

I pray for the day once again your hand I will clutch

Love's Recipe

The Night We Kissed

I reminisce on that night from time to time

Trying to figure out, how did things go wrong

It was a night that will never leave my mind

So special it makes me wish I could go back to that specific time

It was unlike anything I have ever felt

The feeling that went through my body was like being in a coma for some time and finally waking up

It was like being lost in the woods and finally finding your way

It was so strong and passionate, it was like kissing an angel

Something one can only dream about, a kiss that truly defines what love is all about

With that one kiss it was as if everything about you was unveiled to me

Your beauty became even more clear to me, a beauty that I had never seen before

It's as if I had been seeing everything in black and white and that kiss enhanced my vision and upgraded me

Terry L. Ware, Sr.

My heart was racing immensely on my ride home that night

As if I was in shock by what I had just felt

I'd give anything to once again feel that feeling

Because that night my life was transformed with just one kiss

The Perfect Night

The first time we met was like love at first sight

Never thought I believed in it until that night

It was like an angel dropped out of the skies

And fell in my world undisguised

We connected with the first words of hello

I remember it like yesterday, because I stepped on your toe

We laughed and talked all night, never gasping for air

It's like we needed to know everything that night

The time came to say goodnight

But neither wanted to leave one another's sight

I remember laying down that night

And reminiscing on how we gazed in each other's eyes

Like we could see in each other's souls

That was the night

The night I fell in love

Terry L. Ware, Sr.

Through the Clutter

In the midst of a whirlwind
I found love
Through the pains that tore through my skin with an unwillingness to live
I found love
Grazing through the woods, darkness all around, careful where to step for the thorns that implanted themselves in me
I found love
Through bad decisions made, while all along running from my fate
I found love
Through the unhappiness that traveled through my blood
Raging and pounded through my bones
I found love

Through the weakness that consoled my skin, often came out in the form of sin
I found love
Through the hate that corroded my mind, losing track of all things, missing all signs
I found love
In the deepest moments of fear, tears drowning my face, nothing seemed clear
I found love
Breaking free from things that surrounded me, walking through those things that once blinded me
Able to face this situation head on, I had to go through the clutter to find what real love was
I finally have found love

Thoughts of the Heart

As your heart beats, it speaks

As it beats I listen

Softly as a whisper

Gentle as your touch

It says so much

Every word filled

It explains how you truly feel

Not too loud does it speak

The heart is very fragile

You won't hear unless you first seek

The pain runs deep

It's in search

Search of something more

In search of something meaningful

But don't focus in on just that

There's so much more waiting for you to hear

Terry L. Ware, Sr.

It's speaking of love

Not luv, but love

It constantly tells you

Both day and night

But yet you still fight

Fight against everything it's saying

Cause you're not listening

Your own heart you have never heard

You're too busy trying to be a part of the world

You'd rather listen to others

Than to trust something that has been a part of you since day one

Sit still for just a moment

Close your eyes and focus

Block out everything you've ever heard

Now do you hear that

It is your heart speaking

It doesn't speak loud

Love's Recipe

Because that's not what it was designed to do

It was designed to take care of

Nothing happens without the heart first saying that things are ok

Your heart wants to hold a conversation with you

But until you take the time out to listen you will never be able to hear

If you never hear, how can your heart take you in the right direction

Terry L. Ware, Sr.

Where Is Your Protection

You dove right in not thinking twice of the consequence

The feelings that come tell you protection makes no sense

You say you love yourself and would do anything to protect you

Yet risk and risk you take time and time again

You carry yourself like an unrevised email

Instead of taking time out to proof read, you choose to hit send

Unworthy of love is what you portray, not worthy of loving is what you say

Like the wind blows you move from situation to situation

Never taking time to get to know anything, instead you move right along

In one ear and out the other goes the things you need to hear

For doing the right thing and standing for something positive you fear

When it rains you constantly get wet

Love's Recipe

Yet you wonder and many times fear of the consequences from you constantly getting wet

Sickness in your body, pains that could arise but your choice is to still compromise

You are not really scared, in fact I don't think you have any fear

You welcome diseases, trials, and tribulations and even infections

Where oh where is your protection....

Your protection lies within Jesus Christ, He can protect you like no other

Terry L. Ware, Sr.

What's This Feeling

I've tried and tried yet the scent of your love has enchanted my soul

My bones now feel whole and my blood can now flow while my flesh becomes smooth again

My hearing has now become clear and no longer do I taste fear

For my eyes are finally open and the darkness has faded now that I have you

It's as such that I have lost myself within the inner part of you

Your thoughts have become my thoughts to the point where my thinking has enhanced to such that as you think I do

The joys of child birth I could never feel for within a woman that has been sealed

But you have filled within me the joys which brings back the happiness I once felt as a child

The pages of my life have seemed to stop turning and the beginning of my story has now begun

As I write, the words sprout simply because you have cleared a path and I finally know the direction to go

Love's Recipe

Entrapped within this new found feeling scary as it seems I have found the real me

Standing alone no longer will I be, for next to me could be someone I know I will never leave

Such as the winds blow still I stand for what I need to know lies within this feeling

As it ponders I ponder and as it whispers I listen because I desire to know this feeling that resides inside of me

Yet this feeling that I feel I can only pray never leaves me

Terry L. Ware, Sr.

So Amazing

The smile of an angel that lights up your personality

Sets you apart and enhances your sensuality

From the tats on your back to the way you state your facts

To love in your eyes that has me mesmerized

I see past your imperfections I go deeper than your flaws

I understand that you are human, I'll be there if ever you fall

Your style is that of a lady, no questions, if ands or maybes

Your frowns, never sad, but says that you have power

A king by your side, never settling for cowards
Sanitizing your life, breaking free from all germs

Leaving behind lost loves and those that didn't remain firm

Unique in your own way, blessed with much grace

So amazingly wonderful is written all over your face

Love's Recipe

Am I in Love

Why is it that my soul reacts to this feeling in my mind

Why is it that I constantly feel you next to me all the time, yet you are not there

I think more than I probably should of holding you, looking in your eyes, and expressing how much I need you in my life

A breath of fresh air is what you are to me

My future with you in it, is all I seem to see

Blinded, no, shocked, no, just waiting for you to walk into my life as I open the door

Hardship and situations I know will arise, but with you by my side I know above all I will rise

I just can't erase the way I feel, because what I feel is what I've been waiting a lifetime to feel

Somewhere inside I know you too feel the same, that's why I'm not ashamed

To say I am finally in love

Terry L. Ware, Sr.

How Do I Stay

Sitting here entrapped within my own pain

Thinking to myself, why the rain

It seems rainier days lately than sunny

I often sit and laugh to myself though nothing is funny

Laughing within is what I do

To try and keep myself from saying those things I know will hurt you

But true to myself is where I must start

Because only then can I speak from my heart

Most may look at me and feel inside there lies not much pain

But to them I say

Touch my heart

And as it pumps the blood flows

And as it flows so does the pain

And if you hold your hand there long enough

The way my heart pumps, gets rough and rough

Love's Recipe

So many things I've dealt with in life

But I've only dealt with those things and have never dealt with life

Many times I feel as though I'd rather just ask God for a pass

That way this would be all over and my pain would be gone fast

We go through trials, and tribulations to make us strong

Besides what would life be like if the rain never falls

God has granted us the ability of choice

But what gets in our way

Is we fail to hear His voice

So as the pain flows, I pray so does the strength

And either I can sit and complain, and complain

Or I can take a stand

Take Him at His word

And hold on to His unchanging hand

My Queen

I see you for who you are and for what you need, you are my queen

I see your heart's desire, to know you is my job, you are my queen

To read your mind I just can't do, but your every thoughts I promise to hold true, you are my queen

My deepest thoughts I know I can share with you, because inside is where you will keep them, and sacred is what they will be, you are my queen

Through your eyes I see destiny, me and kids to be, you are my queen

You in my life has made me a better person, a better man, and for that I love you, you are my queen

No other woman on this earth could measure to your love

Could amount to your beauty

Or could hold a candle to your personality

No one else could be what you are to me

My queen

Permanent Love

A love that cannot be explained

A love felt deep within your veins

A love that dries your tears

A love that eases all fears

A love that gives you strength

A love that mends

A love that has you thinking constantly

A love that is desperate but waits patiently

A love that takes away the words

A love that fills all voids

A love that hurts but still makes you smile

A love that says this is real

A love that in your heart you finally truly feel

A love that at anytime can set your mind free

A love that is permanent, a love to you from me

Terry L. Ware, Sr.

The Very Essence of a Blessing

The definition of a mother is simple and pure
for without your prayers this life would have been hard to
endure

The strength you've shown throughout my life
was the strength I needed to make it through every hard
strife

The love that runs through your veins
simply put is the love that covered me when in my life it
rained

Many times you worried
but even more times I know you prayed
this is why I am the man that I am today

The very essence of your presence is what showered me
the mere examination you allowed God to do in your life
this is what has examined me

Movement of the hearts earth rotation (mother)
this is what you have been to me
the very core

To still have you in my life
means more than any sacrifice

Love's Recipe

Because of your allowance for God to work through you
your willingness to me to always be true
has shown me what a true woman is

And for that alone
this life I will never fear

I love you now
I love you tomorrow
forever and always
will I love you
you are my mother
and you are on earth second to none!!!!!

Terry L. Ware, Sr.

Love's Recipe

It carries many meanings

To some it has lost its value

Used for wrong, used for good

Yet has never hurt anyone, that I can assure you

For it is we as people that dish out the hurt

Consumed in ourselves thus seeing this as dirt

Recognizing not, what this really consists of

Memory loss not allowing you to see, it came from above

Selfless acts, people that stab you in the back

Known to us as disappointments

These we must accept, for it is part of our growth

Part of our strength

Emotions racing as we suffer through pain

But how would we make it to the next stage if He stopped the rain?

Tribulations and lies, trials that try and keep us down

Loss of affection, feeling imperfections, thus

Love's Recipe

Leaving your face full of disgrace known as

Frowns

Devoting yourself to those that hurt you time and time again

Finding out that those you thought loved you

Were by-standers, camouflaged as friends

Seeking passion from lovers, trading pleasure for pain

Wondering why oh why from pointless relations

Nothing you gain

It is a part of life

Something we just can't live without

We can either take the easy or the hard route

Love isn't what fails you, most of the time it's you!

Wanting to always blame others because you choose to be the fool

Love is oh so simple

Yet we make it so very hard

Love is life and we are the reason for most of our scars

epilogue

Terry L. Ware, Sr.

about the Author

My name is Terry L. Ware Sr. I am the son of Myron and Teresa Moody. I have two children, Aniah, and Terry L. Ware Jr., whom are the joy of my life. I currently reside in Montgomery, AL where I have resided for about 9 years now. I have been writing poetry for a little over 15 years now. When I first started writing I never dreamed of having my own book, I was actually just writing for fun. It wasn't until a few people read some of my work and suggested I do a book one day. Those words are what gave light to me beginning my path to publish my own book of poetry.

I am a poet who is very versatile but I have found that love poetry has captured my heart. I believe love is life and without love, there is no life. In this book my collection of love poems focuses on many different situations of love, from pain, to joy, to disappointments, to the love of God. I am very excited about this book in which it is my very first book. I hope that you enjoy this book as much as I enjoyed putting it together.

Terry L. Ware Sr.

a few words from Terry

Love surrounds us and if we allow it to it captivates us to take us to that man and woman that we were created to be. Love is not something to fear but it should be handled with care. Love itself never hurts us but rather wants to fill us to the point that it overflows from us into the lives of others. Love is God and God is Love. Allow true love to enter your heart and show you what living is all about…

Much Love and Many Blessings

Terry L. Ware Sr.

Connections to Terry

Facebook

www.facebook.com/AuthorTerryWareSr

Website

http://www.authorterrylwaresr.yolasite.com/

Author's Page

http://www.innerchildpress.com/terry-l-ware-sr.php

E-Mail

TerryLWareSr@gmail.com

Inner Child Press

Inner Child Press is a Publishing Company Founded and Operated by Writers. Our personal publishing experiences provides us an intimate understanding of the sometimes daunting challenges Writers, New and Seasoned may face in the Business of Publishing and Marketing their Creative "Written Work".

For more Information

Inner Child Press

www.innerchildpress.com

intouch@innerchildpress.com

www.ingramcontent.com/pod-product-compliance
Lightning Source LLC
Chambersburg PA
CBHW071715090426
42738CB00009B/1784